P9-DGP-988

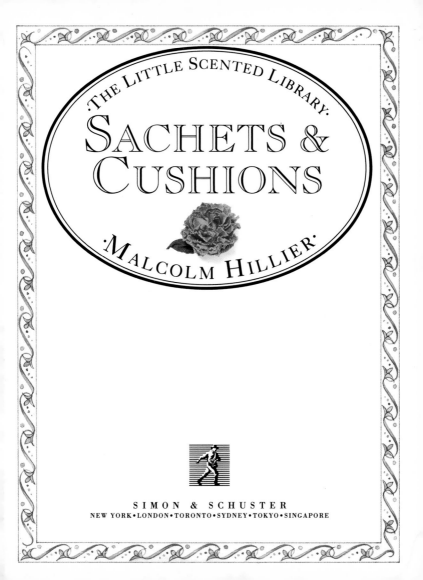

·THE LITTLE SCENTED LIBRARY·

SACHETS & CUSHIONS

·MALCOLM HILLIER·

SIMON & SCHUSTER
NEW YORK•LONDON•TORONTO•SYDNEY•TOKYO•SINGAPORE

A DORLING KINDERSLEY BOOK

SIMON & SCHUSTER
SIMON & SCHUSTER BUILDING, ROCKEFELLER CENTER
1230 AVENUE OF THE AMERICAS, NEW YORK, NY 10020

FIRST PUBLISHED IN GREAT BRITAIN IN 1992
BY DORLING KINDERSLEY LIMITED,
9 HENRIETTA STREET, LONDON WC2E 8PS
PRINTED IN HONG KONG
10 9 8 7 6 5 4 3 2 1

LIBRARY OF CONGRESS CATALOGING-IN-PUBLICATION DATA
IS AVAILABLE ON REQUEST

INCLUDES INDEX

2

CONTENTS

INTRODUCTION

OVER THE LAST FEW years there has been a tremendous revival of interest in herbs. We are learning, once again, to appreciate the culinary and medicinal properties of herbs, and to savor their sweet, potent aromas.

The horticultural definition of herbs includes a wider group of plants than the layman's interpretation of the word. The term derives from the Latin, "herba" a grass, which covers all plants that die down in winter. However, this is rather a broad use of the word, and we tend to think of herbs as plants with distinctive flavors or aromatic foliage.

Most common varieties of herbs can be grown in temperate climates, where the summers are warm and dry, and the winters are fairly mild. They are widely available in shops, but it is satisfying to create a small area devoted to herbs in a sunny corner of the garden, or grow them in containers on the balcony or patio. Whether you grow your own herbs or buy them from a shop, you can fill your home with their aromatic scents, concoct restorative potions and tonics for your skin and hair, and add an intriguing piquancy to your sweet and savory dishes.

DRIED FLOWERS

*M*OST FRAGRANT FLOWERS can be used in potpourris. To make a potpourri, mix dried petals and leaves with spices, essential oils, and a fixative, such as powdered orris root. The quantities will vary, depending on the recipe. Store in a sealed jar for at least six weeks, shaking daily.

Roses *retain a glorious scent when dried.*

Artemisia *is very aromatic. Many varieties have sweet-smelling leaves, stems, and seeds.*

Eucalyptus *has a very pungent perfume allied to mint. Use sparingly in cushions and sachets, as it has an acrid aroma.*

Santolina *flowers and foliage have a sweet scent with overtones of citrus. They are often used in potpourris.*

Bergamot *has highly fragrant leaves and stems. It is used to give Earl Grey tea its special flavor.*

Yarrow *has a pungent, tangy perfume. Delicious mixed with other flowers in potpourris, but use in small quantities.*

Achillea 'Moonshine' *has a sharp scent that is similar to yarrow, but more delicate. Crumble its dried flowers into your fragrant potpourris.*

Wattle, *like mimosa, has golden flowers that continue to emit their sweet, honeyed perfume long after they are dry. It is delicious in light, fresh, lemony potpourris.*

Lavender *has a heady summer fragrance that lasts for years.*

Sneezewort *has a delicate, fresh scent reminiscent of chrysanthemums.*

Peony *has a sweet, buttery perfume that is very long lasting.*

Oakmoss *has a strong perfume redolent of iris. It is often used as a fixative.*

HERBS & SPICES

*A*ROMATIC HERBS and warm, musky spices are the basis of many potpourris, adding a depth and piquancy to fragrant mixes. Many of the spices will also serve as fixatives, helping to preserve the perfumes of the flowers in your potpourri.

Bay *has softly spicy leaves with a highly distinctive scent reminiscent of cloves.*

Oregano *has a similar fragrance to thyme, but is sweeter and more delicate.*

Tansy *has a sharp, tangy summer fragrance with citrus overtones.*

Eucalyptus nuts *are fragrant, but astringent. Use in very small quantities.*

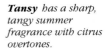

Peppercorns *have a piquant tang and are sharp and spicy when crushed. They are surprisingly aromatic in potpourris.*

Star anise *seeds are aromatic, and have a pungent smell of licorice when crushed. Their starry shapes look decorative in potpourris.*

Santolina has a sharp, astringent tang similar to eucalyptus and lemon.

Sage is deliciously aromatic, but can easily be overpowering if large amounts are used.

Dill has one of the freshest and most subtle scents of all fragrant herbs.

Rosemary, one of the most well known of all aromatic herbs, has a strong, woody fragrance, and mixes well with the flowery scents of roses and peonies in potpourris.

Cinnamon is a delicious foil to perfumed flowers in pot-pourris and is also a fixative.

Nutmeg, when ground, has a scent redolent of honeysuckle, lilies, and tobacco plant flowers.

Saffron is made from the stamens of crocuses and has a delicious, sweet, antiseptic fragrance.

Cloves have a sharp, zingy scent. They are sometimes used as a fixative in potpourris.

CHOOSING FABRICS

*S*ILKS, COTTONS, LINENS, WOOLS —
a wealth of fabrics that spoils
us for choice. As well as the
vast range of materials available, there
is also a multitude of really beautiful
designs in myriad of colors.
Most fabrics are suitable for
making up scented sachets,
pillows, and cushions, but
the size and design of the
finished item dictates the
style and quality of the
fabrics you choose.

FABRIC FANFARE

A broad spectrum of designs, weights, and colors is displayed in this attractive collection of fabrics. The three cotton prints to the left of the group would be suitable for sachets, as these look better made from smaller patterned, finer materials. The four in the center are a mixture of dress and medium-weight furnishing fabrics, and are printed with fairly large, bold designs. These could all be used for a scented cushion or perhaps a sleep pillow. To the right of the group are three heavier furnishing fabrics, ideal for larger cushions or bolsters, as they are thick and hardwearing, yet still allow the soft scent of the potpourri to gently seep through.

11

MAKING A SACHET

OR CENTURIES we have been making floral scented sachets or sweet bags to hang in the linen cupboard and wardrobe or place in our drawers to perfume our clothes. These little bags impart a subtle fragrance to clothing and help to keep moths at bay.

LACY CIRCULAR SACHET
This simple sachet is made from a lightweight floral cotton and is prettily edged with lace. You could either hang it in your wardrobe, or it could nestle among your clothes and linens in a cupboard or chest of drawers.

1 Cut 2 identical circles of a lightweight, floral-printed cotton 4in (10cm) across. With right sides facing outward, stitch the 2 edges together, leaving an opening of approximately 2in (5cm). Spoon the pot-pourri mixture through the opening of the sachet, being careful not to overfill. Sew up the gap.

3 Remove the gathering thread and sew the lace neatly to the sachet. Remove the pins. Make a hanging ribbon loop and sew this to the edge of the sachet. Using the same color ribbon, make a small ribbon bow and sew this to the sachet so that it conceals the end of the ribbon loop.

2 Cut a length of lace twice as long as the circumference of the sachet. Sew running stitches along its length, then gather the lace by pulling the thread. Pin the lace around the edge of the sachet.

FLORAL SACHETS

*M*AKE SACHETS from floral fabrics and fill them with delicate, flowery perfumes. When you prepare your potpourri mixes, try to avoid the stronger oils and essences, and instead rely on the perfumes of the flowers themselves for the fragrance.

BUTTERFLY SACHET
The blue sweet pea design on this butterfly-shaped sachet is enhanced by the flowery perfume of its potpourri. This consists of mixed petals, a light sweet pea oil, ground bay leaves, and some ground tonka beans.

HANGING DIAMOND
A soft, delicate potpourri mix of fragrant rose and peony petals, chopped mint, and powdered orris root, fills this small but decorative hanging sachet.

FUCHSIA SACHET
A mixture of oregano, lemon verbena leaves, rose petals, and powdered orris root fills this stylish sachet, printed with a pretty fuchsia design.

RUFFLED LACE SACHET
A colorful hanging sachet, with a bold, floral pattern of beautiful red auriculas, is edged with a pretty lacy ruff and decorated with a red bow. It contains a sweet-smelling floral mix of fragrant rose petals, ground rosemary and bay leaves, rose oil, and ground tonka beans.

FORGET-ME-NOT HEART
This heart-shaped sachet, with its dainty lace edging and sprigged country rose and forget-me-not pattern, is perfect either for hanging in a wardrobe or for placing in a drawer. The potpourri filling is made from woodruff, pinks and peony petals, ground cloves, and frankincense.

EXOTIC SACHETS

*A*DD A MYSTERIOUS and intriguing perfume to your sachets and sweet bags by including exotic ingredients in your potpourris. There is also a host of oils you can add which, if used in small quantities, will give a pleasing, but not too overpowering, fragrance. Try the light, fresh fragrances of lemon verbena and lemon-scented geranium leaves or the soft, flowery oils of heliotrope, orange blossom, bergamot, tuberose, and gardenia. For a heavier scent, use the woody essences of cedar and sandal.

MOON SACHET
This small, fragrant, moon-shaped sachet contains an exotic mix of 12 tablespoons of fragrant rose petals, 1 tablespoon of ground pine tips, 3 ground eucalyptus seeds, ½ teaspoon of ground cloves, and 2 tablespoons of oakmoss.

ROSY SCENTS

This fine cotton voile, printed in moody, autumn colors and striped with a satin rust piping, is sewn up into an attractive diamond-shaped sachet. Its intriguing perfume is made from 16 tablespoons of rose petals, 4 crushed cardamom seeds, 1 drop of patchouli oil, 2 drops of vanilla oil, and 1 teaspoon of storax.

JAZZY BAG

A circle of shocking pink, blue, and mustard printed cotton is filled with a delicious, spicy potpourri and tied with bright pink and gold ribbons. The fragrant potpourri filling is made from 5 tablespoons each of peony petals, larkspur, and lemon-scented geranium leaves, 1 drop each of bergamot oil and heliotrope oil, and 1 teaspoon of powdered orris root.

MAKING A CUSHION

*C*USHIONS NOT ONLY ADD a decorative touch to a room, but they are a necessity if you have uncomfortable chairs! If you add some potpourri to the cushion stuffing, you can enjoy the delicate fragrance as you relax in your chair. Try to make the scented filling reflect the material of the cushion, just as the cushion should reflect the mood of your room.

SUMMER-SCENTED CUSHION
The summery design of this pretty cushion is echoed in the fragrance of the potpourri filling. This is made from a mixture of 7 tablespoons each of mixed petals and mint, and 1 teaspoon each of ground cloves and powdered orris root.

1 To make the cushion, cut out 2 squares of plain fabric. With right sides facing, sew 3 of the edges together. Turn the cushion out and fill with stuffing mixed with about 8 tablespoons of scented potpourri. Alternatively, put the potpourri into a muslin bag, making it easier to replace. Sew up the fourth side.

2 For the cover, cut out 2 identical squares of fabric, each slightly larger than the cushion, and a narrow piece of the same fabric for the frill. Pleat the frill and sew it to the edges of one of the squares. With right sides facing, sew the squares together around 3 of the sides and turn the cover out. Insert the cushion.

3 To finish, sew a few press studs along the fourth edge. When the perfume of the potpourri begins to fade, open the cushion cover and renew the filling inside.

SPICY CUSHIONS

*S*INCE TIME IMMEMORIAL, spices have been highly valued for their intriguing flavors and exotic aromas. There is still a mysterious and exciting ring to the word "spice." It conjures up the bustle of an oriental market, and evokes the colors and intensity of hot, noonday shadows.

FLORAL TAPESTRY
The warm, burnt colors of seeds and bark are echoed in this exquisite fabric, resembling the tapestries of old. The spicy filling is made from rose petals, ground cinnamon, rosewood oil, and frankincense.

ORIENTAL FRAGRANCE

The soft, natural colors and bold, geometric designs of the carpets and kilims of the Middle East are the inspiration for this richly patterned cushion. The thickness of the fabric allows the spicy perfume to filter through, while ensuring that the fragrance is not dissipated too quickly. I have combined mixed petals with ground coriander, cloves, nutmeg, and allspice, crushed eucalyptus seeds, crushed aniseed, and ground tonka beans, in this exotic mixture.

COTTAGE CUSHIONS

*P*RETTY COTTON CUSHIONS with country designs of flowers, fruits, and ribbons are delightful filled with floral potpourris. Collect a variety of scented petals from the garden and give your house a summertime fragrance all year round.

FRILLED OVAL CUSHION
This attractive frill-edged chintz cushion is filled with a light, floral potpourri mixture of ground nutmeg, pink peony petals, white larkspur, lemon geranium oil, hops, and powdered orris root.

WILD STRAWBERRIES
For this cushion, covered with a pattern of trailing wild strawberries, I have chosen a mixture made from lemon verbena leaves, rose petals, larkspur, crushed cardamoms, and gum benzoin.

ROSE MIX
This traditional circular cushion, with a central bow, is covered in a delicate chintz print of interweaving pink ribbons. It contains a mix of fragrant rose petals, pink campion, ground cinnamon, and oakmoss.

MAKING A PILLOW

*I*T IS A GREAT LUXURY to have a gently scented bedroom. Perfumed pillows release a soft, subtle fragrance into the room, and are attractive and simple to make. Ensure that you use a very mild potpourri, exuding just a hint of perfume.

1 Fill the inner pillow case with some stuffing and 8 tablespoons of mild pot~pourri. Select fabric and bows for the pillow case.

2 Cut 2 pieces of your chosen fabric slightly larger than the inner pillow. Hold the right sides firmly together and stitch carefully along the 2 longer sides, leaving the shorter ends open. Press open the seams and turn out the pillow case.

3 Fold over and stitch a narrow double hem at each end or bind the raw edges with bias binding or ribbon. Press. Use ribbon to make the ties, or alternatively, you could make them from the same fabric, as shown here. Attach these to the inside of the pillow case, slip the cover over the scented inner pillow, and keep it in position by tying bows securely at both ends.

SCENTED PILLOW

Lemon verbena is the fragrant base of this mildly scented pillow, but alternatively, you could use roses, chamomile, or lavender. Mix 4 tablespoons each of oregano and lemon verbena leaves with 7 tablespoons of mixed petals and 1 tablespoon of powdered orris root. 8 tablespoons of this potpourri is quite sufficient to perfume an average-sized pillow.

SCENTED BOLSTERS

*B*OLSTERS ARE LONG, narrow cushions or pillows that are attractive soft furnishings and can be used as supports. Placed across the corner of a sofa or at the end of a *chaise longue*, a bolster provides excellent support for the lower back. Alternatively, bolsters can be displayed decoratively on a bed or even used as draught excluders. They are best covered in a furnishing fabric or in a combination of fabrics, as here. To add a subtle fragrance, slip a sachet of potpourri into the stuffing.

ELEGANT BOLSTER

*This distinctive, softly coloured bolster is made
using two complementary pieces of fabric sewn in
bands. The ends are sealed with rope and tassels. It is
stuffed with a firm kapok filling and I have added a small
muslin bag containing a fragrant potpourri. For a delicate
country garden perfume, blend 4 tablespoons
each of fragrant rose and peony petals with
2 tablespoons each of lavender, chamomile,
marjoram, and oregano, 2 drops of
bergamot oil, and 1 teaspoon of powdered
orris root. If you intend to use the bolster
in a bedroom, I suggest that you do
not include the lavender and bergamot
oil in the potpourri mix, as they emit quite
a strong fragrance, which may be too
pungent for some people.*

SLEEP PILLOWS

BLACK AND WHITE is a particularly striking combination for bed linen. These pillows are highly decorative and, if filled with a delicate blend of herbs and flowers, they can soothe you with their scents and help you sleep more easily and more deeply.

SWEET DREAMS
This stylish sleep pillow is made from an intriguing, richly patterned, floral cotton print. It contains a softly perfumed potpourri made from a mixture of fragrant rose petals, rosemary leaves, and powdered orris root.

STRIPED ELEGANCE
This striped pillow contains a pot-pourri of fragrant marjoram, rose petals, bergamot, lavender, and ground tonka beans.

CLASSICAL STYLE
The ornate patterns of wrought ironwork are the inspiration for this striking print. Notice how the strong black architectural motifs stand out against the stark white background. The pillow is filled with a potpourri of lemon verbena, scented rose petals, hops, and powdered orris root.

BOUQUET GARNIS

*S*PICES AND AROMATIC HERBS lend a piquancy to most savory dishes, including soups, broths, stews, and sauces. Bound in small muslin sachets known as bouquet garnis, they are quick and easy to make. They impart an aromatic, herby savor to food during cooking, but should be removed before or during serving.

AROMATIC DISHES

To make a bouquet garni, cut out a piece of muslin 6in (15cm) across and place some herbs and spices in the center. Gather the bundle together and tie it with thread or raffia. Bay, parsley, and thyme are the most usual ingredients for a bouquet garni, but you can combine any herbs and spices you choose. Try an aromatic blend of lemon peel, parsley, celery leaf, cardamom, and saffron with rice dishes; for fish stews, I like to use juniper, star anise, lime, parsley, and dill. Far Eastern dishes are enhanced by a bouquet garni of basil, chives, Szechuan pepper, chili, peppercorns, oregano, and bay. For lamb, you could try bay leaves, rosemary, peppercorns, crushed garlic, and orange peel.

SCENTED PINCUSHIONS

WE CAN MAKE our work so much more enjoyable if we surround ourselves with bright colors and soft scents. A cheerful pincushion filled with a potpourri filling is always a delight to have on hand.

NEEDLEWORKER'S COMPANIONS

Mixes of rose petals, juniper, artemisia, cloves, and ground tonka beans give these pincushions a summery fragrance. Pincushions are a very practical way to use up any leftover pieces of fabric. The heart-, diamond-, and apple-shaped pincushions shown here are, in fact, all made from sections of the same colorful material.

MAKING A PINCUSHION

1 Cut out 2 heart-shaped pieces of fabric. With right sides facing, stitch the edges together, leaving a small opening.

2 Turn right sides out and stuff with a mixture of kapok and 3 tablespoons of potpourri. Sew up the gap and decorate with a bow.

BATH SACHETS

*T*HERE IS NOTHING MORE SOOTHING than a long, self-indulgent soak in a warm, deliciously scented bath. Sachets containing flowers or herbs are a delightful way to perfume the bath water, and are very easy to make. Loop a sachet over the hot tap, so the water runs through the bag, and enjoy the fragrance of the scented water.

HERBAL BATH SACHETS

To make herbal bath sachets, mix a tablespoon each of chopped fresh or dried herbs and oatmeal or dried milk powder, and add some fragrant rose petals. Wrap them in muslin and tie the bundle with ribbon, allowing for a loop at the top for hanging. A great variety of herbs are suitable for using in the bath, most of which are not only fragrant, but are also known for their curative and restorative properties. Mint and rosemary are thought to invigorate the body and mind, while marjoram eases rheumatic pain and tension; tarragon is used as a very effective skin toner, and I would recommend bay to soothe away the aches and pains of the long day. Lemon verbena, chamomile, and lime blossoms are also soothing, and will fill your bathroom with their delicate perfumes.

35

EVENING BAGS

*A*N ELEGANT evening bag was an essential accessory for any Victorian lady. These bags were often made from truly exquisite fabrics, and were sometimes embellished with delicate hand embroidery, glass beads, or rich gold braiding. Some bags were scented, containing an inner "pocket" that would contain a potpourri. Make your own scented bags, and fill them with fragrant petals or oriental spices.

MAKING A SCENTED BAG

1 Cut 2 identical pieces of fabric. Fold both pieces in half to make 2 bags. With right sides facing, stitch along 2 sides. Turn out 1 bag. Turn over and baste the top of each bag. Put 1 bag inside the other and slip potpourri between the 2 bags.

2 Stitch the 2 bags together at the top. Cut 2 thin strips of fabric and hem each strip. Stitch the strips to the bag, leaving the short ends open. Cut 2 lengths of cord and thread through the strips from opposite directions. Tie the ends.

EMBROIDERED PURSE

A striped moiré fabric is made into a stylish drawstring purse and decorated with a bud motif. It is filled with a softly scented potpourri of summer flowers.

QUILTED BAG

A heart-shaped bag for a Valentine's Day ball is made from a fine golden damask, finished with gold braiding. It is filled with lemon verbena and oakmoss.

SPICY POUCH

Both sides of this stunning fabric have been used for this chic evening purse. It is filled with a lightly spicy potpourri mix of bergamot, nutmeg, and powdered orris root.

FRAGRANT INFUSIONS

A GREAT VARIETY OF INFUSIONS are available in the shops nowadays, but I think home-made brews are the most delicious. Simply place a blend of fruits, flowers, and tea if you wish, in a 6in (15cm) square of muslin, tie the bundle, and steep the sachet in a teapot or cup for four to five minutes.

VIOLETS & ORANGE
This is an unusual but really delicious brew. Blend fragrant violets and a few slivers of tangy orange peel with a teaspoon of Darjeeling tea.

ROSEHIPS & ROSE PETALS
Rosehips and rose petals have a fine, flowery flavor and make an excellent beverage. Here, they are mixed with a teaspoon of Keemun tea to make a delicate, highly perfumed infusion.

APPLES & MINT

Dried apples and finely chopped apple mint can be blended with a teaspoon of Darjeeling tea for a very refreshing brew. I like to drink this with a little sugar.

PEACH & PEACH BLOSSOM

Dried peaches have a sweet but subtle flavor. Chopped finely and placed in a sachet with some Oolong Peach Blossom tea, they make a delicate, fruity infusion that is always delicious.

ELDERBERRIES & HIBISCUS

Elderberries have a highly distinctive flavor. Crushed and mixed with some hibiscus blossoms, they make a sweet-smelling infusion that is soothing, refreshing, and caffeine-free. In the summer, you could substitute fresh elderflowers for the dried elderberries.

INDEX

ACKNOWLEDGMENTS

The author would like to thank
Quentin Roake for all his help in producing
this book, and Sheila Coulson for making
the cushions, sachets, pillows, and
bags that appeared in this book.

Dorling Kindersley would like
to thank Pauline Bayne, Polly Boyd,
Gill Della Casa, Jillian Haines,
Mary-Clare Jerram, and
Caroline Webber.